That's Not a Fishing Boat, It's a Giraffe: Responses to Austerity

Ian McMillan

smith|doorstop

Published 2019 by Smith|Doorstop Books
The Poetry Business
Campo House,
54 Campo Lane,
Sheffield S1 2EG
www.poetrybusiness.co.uk

ISBN 978-1-912196-75-3
Designed & Typeset by Utter
Printed by Biddles

Acknowledgements

Thanks to the producers and editors of the following, where some of these poems first appeared: BBC Radio 4, Hardship anthology, the Giant Steps anthology.

Smith|Doorstop books are a member of Inpress: www.inpressbooks.co.uk. Distributed by NBN International, Airport Business Centre, 10 Thornbury Road Plymouth PL 6 7PP.

The Poetry Business gratefully acknowledges the support of Arts Council England.

Contents

Channel

Welcome, in your tiny boats.
Here is a gold piano
For you to rest in.

Welcome, with your soaking clothes.
Here is a butler's pocket
For you to sleep in.

Chart

In the opticians. A man comes in, says

THEY SHOULD SEND THEM ALL BACK
THEY SHOULD SEND THEM ALL BACK
THEY SHOULD SEND THEM ALL BACK
THEY SHOULD SEND THEM ALL BACK
THEY SHOULD SEND THEM ALL BACK
THEY SHOULD SEND THEM ALL BACK
THEY SHOULD SEND THEM ALL BACK

That special intimacy of the opticians.
The way they look into your eyes. His
Bald head gleamed in weak winter sun.
He could read all the way down to the bottom
And beyond, if there had been more words.

In the Barber's

In the Barber's an older bloke sits in the chair,
Takes his hearing aids out and says
'Yer can seh what yer want nar. Ah can't hear yer.'

The young lad keeps blowing
His grandad's referee's whistle, and the barber
Does the old Tony Curtis/Yul Brynner gag

And a man puts his head round the door
With an 80th birthday card for someone
Who's just been and gone. The lad blows

The whistle. The bloke with the hearing aids out
Shouts 'Men dee afoor women. On a 52-seater coach,
You'll hev 40 women and 12 men.' 'You're all offside'

Says the lad with the whistle. 'That one's disallowed.'

Eight Poems Translated from a Lost Language

1.

The banks of steel flowers are rusting
In the air that was borrowed
From yesterday's mist. Milk seethes
In bottles.

2.

Sing me the end of your song
Before the beginning, said the official,
Officially. I refused. His rope curled.

3.

Sing, unbuilt wall!
Sing, unmade bed!
Sing, untold story!
Sing, uncarried infant in the arms of the uncle!

4.

The sunrise reminds us
That nothing is permanent
Not even the way we speak
As a door slams in our faces.

5.

Your breasts
Are so beautiful
I wish
You had three.

6.

I caught you thinking
By the well. You were thinking
About the well.

Why do you not think
About the sky?
I asked.

The moon is in the well,
You replied.

7.

They said that one day our language would die
And I pointed to a bird and said 'Birdsong never dies,
It just swims from the beak to the ear.'

8.

One line is not a poem unless the king writes it.

Covent Garden and the Bald-Headed Bloke in the T-Shirt.

This flyer brings the past rushing back to me in a huge emotional wave;
I remember the day vividly, the sense that we were poets and performers
against the government, against the establishment, for the striking miners, for
anybody who raised a voice in protest. What I remember most, though, is the
fact that life just swirled around us as we stood and ranted and rapped and
sang and were lyrical and funny and (we hoped) profound.

One man in particular stands out: he was a little bloke with a bald head and
he was wearing a t-shirt that said I'M NOT BALD THIS IS A SOLAR
PANEL FOR A SEX MACHINE and people kept referring to it from the
stage and taking the mickey but he didn't care. He represented all we despised
but he kept coming back for more grief. It just reminds me how polarised the
1980s were.

Drizzle and Traffic and that Seagull

I wek up at four. Pit time.
Pigeon playing its one note song
In the garden. Ovver and ovver.

And three things appear
In my heead. Postcards.
From a past that comes back sometimes.

Fust 'un: that drizzle kissing me cap,
That old lass with no brolly
And me offering me coyt in't bus queue.
She said ta.

Second 'un: that lass wi a babby in a pram
And cars shooitin darn that bypass.
And me stopping 'em while she crossed.
She said thanks mister.

Third 'un: that seagull lying in't gutter
In that freezing summer.
I put it in a wastebin with what was left of me chips.
And it said nowt.

So mebbe change is possible.
In the drizzle and the speeding traffic
And the seagull in the wastebin

That said nowt.

Good to See They've Put the Minimum Wage Up

Spokesman says, reading from notes, at the podium, nice touch that pocket square, nice touch those cufflinks, nice touch the hint of whiskers missed just below the nose in the hasty shave before facing the press,

'We are pleased to announce a rise in the minimum wage. Due to extreme trading conditions the wages will not be paid monetarily but in the form of:

Notes to the milkman, squirrel droppings, drawings of submarines done by prisoners on Death Row, kettles from the recently bankrupted chain KETTLES, nose-balaclavas, English to Welsh phrasebooks, tablecloths, tickets to see Phantom of the Opera at the Queen's Theatre Hornchurch, bottles of Tizer the Appetizer, wooden clothes pegs, shoelaces, canisters of laughing gas, copies of The Holy Bible, KitKats, tricycle wheels, cans of mackerel, cans of Mackeson, support tights one size fits all, bagpipe CDs, jigsaws of Stockport's skyline, jars of homemade chutney, birdboxes, bowler hats and ferrules'.

Spokesman stops speaking. Is overcome with emotion. Whether laughter or tears is difficult to tell. Wipes his eyes with his pocket square. Nice touch that.

Hang

A charity shop coat hanger
Holding the past
And a possible future
In equal measure,

Singing an anthem
Of circular capital
Flying from M&S
Over to Wombwell

And making a landing
Behind possibility
Over by blue high heels'
Tottering history,

Telling their story.
Nobody's listening.

Penny

Monocle-gleam on the pavement,
Fallen moon. Joyce bent to grab it,
Frank leaned over, trying to pick it up,
Jostled Joyce who fell into Satnam
Who was reaching over with a magnet
And Dylan who had put some Blu-tak
On a stick to try and stick it and get it.

Round copper O on the pavement,
Long-dead sun. Satnam thought he'd
Got it and so did Frank, who laughed
Like a rusty hinge just as Joyce,
Losing her footing in the penny-lust,
Fell into them all, skittled them sideways
Leaving Dylan to hold it up to the air,

The cold air that stunk like a bastard.

The Food Bank in the Primary School

A food bank opens in a primary school in Norfolk, December 2018

O Tins of beans beside those little infant chairs!
O Deputy Head bringing pasta in an Aldi bag!
O Reading corner where soup is stored because everybody donates soup!
O Children with faces that belong to their grandparents!
O Unforgiving gulls circling the playground!
O Single tin of raspberries like a cartoon sunset!
O Stray hairs in the nose of the uncle sent with carriers!
O Bright paintings by Year Two children in vivid colours!
O Girl in her brother's shoes!
O Sums you are needed here! You are needed here!
O Children who thought this was a role-playing area!
O Teachers who wished this was a role-playing area!
O Past sell-by date the NQT saw and didn't say!
O Rain beginning to fall just before home-time!
O School caretaker sweeping up spilled sugar!
O Dinner lady weeping into the parts of her pinny she can reach!
O Parents forming a patient queue with the odd tired jostle!
O Spider on the ceiling observing this facet of civilisation!
O Year Six girl helping to carry heavy boxes. Heavy things.
O Skipping reception children!
O Tory MP standing for a photo opportunity with his donation!
O Tory MP standing for a photo opportunity with his donation!
O Tory MP standing for a photo opportunity with his donation!

The Hard Ship

This is the moment just before it is launched
Into the hard water; the hard air is waiting,
Tense as an ironing board just before
The ironing begins. We do as we are told,
We gather, closer and closer to the hull,
Nearer to the water than it is safe to be.

We have seen these Hard Ship launches before:
The dignitaries, the brass band, the speeches
That cannot be heard above the weeping. Fish mouths
Opening and closing, opening and closing.
Stand closer to the Hard Ship! They shout
And we shuffle forward, weeping. We have seen

People crushed by the Hard Ship before, and pushed
Into the hard water where they flail a little, then settle.

Unflappable

1.

Even the strongest breeze
Can't flap that flag;
Even the brightest glare
Can't close that eye.

2.

Here's me with my picker-upper
Picking litter in the morning.
Amongst the usual McDonalds and Costa
Suspects I'm finding more and more
Empty blister packs of tablets,
Chemical voids scattered
Across the pavement's flat-top.
Pain, ache, hurt, *winces*.

3.

A man comes out of the shop
With the word GAS on his back;
Evolution personified.

4.

Even the fastest train
Can't bring me back.
Even the biggest bell
Can't wake me up.

My Austerity Face

Here it is, look. Botoxed
And battered to the side
Of my head like a fish
That has both eyes
On the same side of its
Head. Bleeding lip, fat
Lip. Eyes reduced to red cabbage
By blubbering. Gob like a shut
Library door. Boarded up,
And here, here's an image for yer:
Somebody's left a library book
Outside the shut library: what
Book? What book? A Brief History
Of Time. All over my face.

The Fragility of History

Clang of the pie-and-pea man's bell,
George Street, Friday night, 1980.
He parks. I walk out with two bowls
And he fills them up. The pit bus

Rolls by and the men gesture at me
In a complex series of movements
That can be interpreted as 'Giz
Some of that bastard pie and peas!'

I wave. At this moment none of us know
That this is the last time I will visit
The pie and pea man's clanging bell
With my bowls that shine innocently.

I can't recall if something happened
To me or him, or the van, or the bowls,
Or the pie, or the peas, or the streetlights
Or the stars, or the pit bus, or the universe.

Plain

Each hotel bar is a cardboard cutout of loneliness;
Each bag of crisps opened to reveal more crisps

Then less crisps. Finally no crisps at all. Where's
Your key card, McMillan? Next to your phone again?

Then it won't work. You won't be able to get in.
Look at those two, watching darts on their iPad.

Look at the barman, studying his phone, grinning.
Look at that giant snail in that picture on the wall.

I'll have more crisps then. Make a night of it.
Might buy some for the snail, for the barman,

For the couple cheering a bulls eye. Plain.
I like plain. I like plain. I like plain.

Steam is Ghost Ice

In this kitchen, at this hour,
I am peeling potatoes,
Trying my best to get one long string or cravat of peel
From one tatie.

It is lucky,
One long belt or B-road or headscarf of peel
From a potato. My luck is out.
I'm like a migrating bird

Held at traffic lights
Waiting for something to change.

In a Held Steadiness of Light

I notice that my bitten nails
Cannot be seen in my hands' shadows,
Like you can't see the thoughts under somebody's hat.
It's an improvement, I guess,
On Elsie the cleaner reading out the verses
Of Sympathy cards in the shop, her voice
As faint as a memory of Rin Tin Tin
From my childhood afternoons.
Why is it an improvement?
Because you couldn't really hear her words
Over the songs on Co-op Radio,
But you could watch her lips move,
But you couldn't see my nails
In the shadows.

Nancy

My mother (Sing Something
Simple is on, Jack Emblow's
Accordion slicing through Sunday)

Looks up from Woman's Own
Which half covers her face,
So she is almost like the Woman's

Own cover Woman, and says
'If you'd have been a girl
We were going to call you Nancy'

And I often think about Nancy,
How she would have been grey
Now, like me, how she would

Have enjoyed seeing that little wren
Hop like feathered punctuation
Into that tree. Nancy, Nancy,

Nancy: you may have dreamed
About being Ian. You may have
Looked at your watch and thought

'If time is a human construct
Then why does it hurt so much?'

Somebody Spoke and

somebody
spoke and

The man with the trout
Tattooed on his back
Took off his shirt.
The trout swam away

Into The Vagueness
That's waiting with bells
At the edge of every long afternoon.

Everybody spoke
And we all knew we were
On the bus from the song
A Day In The Life
By The Beatles.

Tent
Event

Let's call him John. John.
Names have been changed to protect
The incontinent

Of speech. John's tent
Is about to welcome a bottle of piss
Chucked

By what newspapers still insist
On calling a 'reveller'. Revel
In this image:

The bottle turning and turning.
John's tent by the cash machine.
Both held in midnight streetlight.

If there's a soundtrack
It's this floor filler.

Evening Match. Floodlights On.

This. I step into the light, literally
Into the view of a pitch laid out like a stage set,
And the game might be forgettable,
Could be a nil-nil draw that drags like mud
But on this night, in this glaringly
Brilliant illumination, the Tuesday air wet
With grudging, chuntering Barnsley drizzle,
I am in the shining middle of something good.
A plane makes its blinking way slowly
Down to the airport. The new moon's slight
Curve mirrors the path of the ball's unstoppable
Passage to the net like a heart pumps blood.
It's moments like this when all the stars align.
Evening games in winter; a touch of the sublime.

Neil Armstrong Leaps

Like a raindrop bouncing
From the surface of a road,
Like a cat jumping
At a wren in a hedge,
Like an idea tangoing
From his head to ours
About distance, and closeness
And the amount of air
We all need to leap in.

Uncle Charlie's Moon

I recall this: his braces
Like a kind of punctuation
Down his shirt. His cap, flat
As a pit pond. His anger.

He points at the distant
Bike lamp of the moon.
'They're nivver theer,
Ian lad. Nivver.' He shakes

His head, coughs, spits.
He can't hear Buzz Aldrin
Shouting 'Charlie! We're here!'
But I can, Charlie. I can.

Fruit Solar System

This big blood orange is the sun, here,
In the middle of the carpet. I've moved the settee
To the outer fringes, near the door.

Mercury you are a tiny redcurrant. So small
You might step on it and then
We'd all be in trouble. So small, Mercury.

Crab Apple Venus. You are bitter and hard
And you turn, turn, turn like chucked fruit.
Earth: I think you are an Egremont Russet

Only because I like Egremont Russets
And I like Earth. Mars you are a cherry
And can people live on a cherry? Well,

I think they might. Jupiter is a grapefruit
But a grapefruit so big you'd have to get
Your mate Harry to help you carry it home.

Me and Geoff Stables and the Can of Beans

Sudden crashing noise as Geoff hurls the can.
Sudden crashing noise as I hurl the can. Dust
Clears. Geoff shakes his head. 'Still there,'

He says, disappointment rusting his voice.
Sudden crashing noise as I hurl the can. Sudden
Crashing noise as Geoff hurls the can into the

Sand. Our summer plan, in 1966's stained glass
August, to chuck a can of beans so hard, so very hard,
Into a pile of sand that it burst the thin socks

Of time and flew into the future. Or the past.
We were fans of science fiction and we were ten.
The world seemed full to the brim of, let's call 'em,

Possibilities. Sudden crashing noise as Geoff hurls
The can. Sudden crashing noise as I hurl the can.
And of course, the beans never slipped into last week

Or next year. *Except, reader, this morning I found
A tin of beans on the shelf WHERE NO BEANS WERE
BEFORE. WHERE NO BEANS WERE BEFORE. Put that*

In your memory and spin it. Sudden crashing noise.

Our Transport Correspondent Speaks

Platform 1

Today's announcement of delays
Is delayed. And now plans well made
Are, well, unmade. The platform tannoy

Crackles into brief life to regret
The delayed delay that pushes today
Into yesterday. The wrong kind

Of customers turned up on time
Committing what the operators
See as the crime of believing the timetable.

Remember: it's a piece of fantasy fiction
Set on a distant planet where
The carriages are clean
And the train companies care.

Platform 2

Bloke on train cleans his ear with a pen in the shape of a carrot.

Bloke on train snores so rhythmically the other passengers sing along.

Bloke on train is reading his newspaper upside down as though.

Bloke on phone on train: I'll tell you this. Keith shouldn't be allowed near one of those.

Bloke on train glugs lager from a tin, kissing it like he's always loved it.

Bloke on train to his neighbour: where do you get those ties? My dad likes them.

Bloke on phone on train: I'll tell you this. Keith's always in Dover in his head.

Bloke on train punches the book he's reading as though he's solved a mystery.

Bloke on phone on train: I'll tell you this. Take everything Keith says with a pinch of rice.

Bloke on train: That grey-haired bloke is writing down everything I say.

Platform 3

In this carriage we
Stand crushed like this into the ribs
Of the woman who is pressed so hard
Into the door
That she will leave an impression there
When she finally gets off,
Like a fossil leaf in a seam of coal.

In this carriage we
Stand so close to each other
That we may as well be married
Or at least engaged. This intimacy
With breath, aftershave, sweat and
The hairs coming out of the ears
Of that man with the moustache
Is a special intimacy. Train intimacy,
Scientists call it. I'd laugh
If there was room to open my mouth.

In this carriage we
Try to keep our own space sacred
Like saints in stained glass windows
Not looking at the other saints
In the same stained glass window.

Three Dreams Rendered Prosaically

1.

It has been announced that the world will end tomorrow because an asteroid is going to crash into the earth. Our children are small and we decide to spend our last evening together watching a video, so we go to Blockbuster in Wombwell and hire one and when I ask the boy behind the counter when we should bring it back he says, in a deep and sonorous voice 'You don't need to bring it back' and we all begin to weep.

2.

I meet David Cameron at an event and he tells me how much he enjoys listening to my Radio 3 show The Verb. I thank him but tell him that I'm not a Conservative voter and indeed I'm a Labour voter and he says 'That's fine but Conservatives can listen to your radio programmes.' I wake up.

3.

A general election has been called and I am walking round Darfield handing daffodils to candidates. I give a daffodil to Theresa May, who accepts it. I give a daffodil to Jeremy Corbyn, who accepts it. I see Nigel Farage leaning on the same wall I used to lean on when I waited for the school bus. I offer him a daffodil and he says 'I'd like to accept your daffodil but as you know daffodils aren't allowed on buses.' A bus comes. He gets on it. I stand there with my daffodils.